PRAYING FOR OUR PRIESTS

A GUIDE TO PRAYING FOR THE PRIESTHOOD
IN UNION WITH
MARY, QUEEN OF THE CLERGY

Thank you for all of your support.
May God continue to Bless you in all that you do.

Fr. John Neneman

Dc. Jose Ferreras

INCLUDES MEDITATIONS ON THE PRIESTHOOD
FOR THE MYSTERIES OF THE ROSARY
AND THE STATIONS OF THE CROSS

BY MONSIGNOR PETER DUNNE
AND VICKI HEROUT

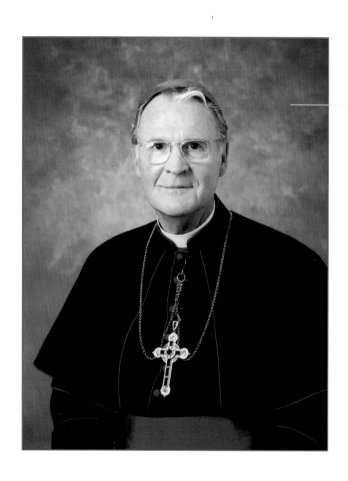

ARCHDIOCESE OF OMAHA

Office of the Archbishop

100 North 62nd Street
Omaha, Nebraska 68132

October 20, 2008

Dear Reader,

This booklet, "Holy Hour for Priests," which was created with the dual purpose of supporting priests and increasing vocations to the ministerial priesthood, is a treasured gift to the Archdiocese of Omaha and to the universal Church.

I found the meditations on the Holy Rosary and the other prayers compiled to accompany Eucharistic adoration to be an appropriate response to the request recently made by Cardinal Claudio Hummes, prefect of the Congregation for Clergy, when he exhorted bishops around the world to bring about in the Church "a movement of prayer, placing 24 hour continuous Eucharistic adoration at the centre…with the primary intention of awakening a sufficient number of holy vocations to the priestly state and, at the same time, spiritually uniting with a certain spiritual maternity…all those who have already been called to the ministerial priesthood…."

It is my hope that this booklet of prayers be distributed in strategic locations throughout the archdiocese and beyond so that the words of Cardinal Hummes may be realized, "This movement will offer better service to Christ and his brothers…standing in Christ's stead and representing him, as head, shepherd and spouse of the Church."

I am sincerely yours in the Lord,

+Elden Curtiss

Most Reverend Elden F. Curtiss
Archbishop of Omaha

Imprimatur: Most Reverend Elden F. Curtiss
              Archbishop of Omaha
              October 1, 2008
              Omaha, Nebraska

Nihil Obstat: Fr. Joseph Taphorn
              Censor Librorum
              Archdiocese of Omaha

ISBN - 10:   0-615-30780-9
ISBN - 13: 978-0-615-30780-0

Dedication: To Mary, Queen of the Clergy

Cover Image:

The image of Our Lady of Victory was chosen for the cover of this booklet because it so beautifully manifests Mary's loving tenderness and solicitude for Her Son, Jesus, Who is the Eternal High Priest. Her tenderness and solicitude for Him extends itself to include every priest son for all time and eternity.

Photography:

Bob Ervin — Ervin Photography; Front & back cover • Crucifix, page 45 • The Stations of the Cross.

Alida Choat — Alida's Picture Pages; The Resurrection, page 64.

Book Design:

Patrick J. Ervin — Ervin and Smith Advertising / Public Relations

TABLE OF CONTENTS

1

PRAYER TO "DIVINE LOVE" FOR PRIESTLY CHARITY

O Divine Love, we come before You to pray and intercede for our priests that they may become the living presence of Your love among us.

O Divine Love, enter and take complete possession of their hearts that all their affections may be toward charity.

O Divine Love, enter and be ever first in their minds that all their thoughts may be charitable.

O Divine Love, enlighten their intellects that they may always discern that which is most charitable.

O Divine Love, imbue all their words that they may always speak that which is most charitable and encouraging.

O Divine Love, inhabit their wills that they may always will and do that which is most charitable.

Divine Love, animate all their senses and movements that they may only hear and see with Your senses and always respond with Your charity.

O Divine Love, penetrate to the very core of their souls, consume all their darkness, until You, O Divine Love, are able to radiate pure love through them to all they meet.

O Mary, Mother of Divine Love, pray for our priests.

INTRODUCTION

There can be no more fruitful investment in the life of Holy
Mother Church than time spent in prayer for Her priests and
vocations to the priesthood.

This project had its origin in the early days of 2006 when
Monsignor Peter Dunne, recovering from a long and critical
illness, experienced a deepening awareness of the need to
pray for his brother priests in Purgatory. At the same time,
Vicki Herout, his longtime caregiver, spiritual daughter, and
coworker in many projects, began to realize in her own prayers
an intense and persistent call to pray for the priesthood.
Eventually, they brought together a group that has continued
to meet regularly to pray for priests. This booklet, initially
compiled as an aid to this prayer group, has been adapted
for use by individuals as well as small and large groups in
a variety of settings.

The meditations on the priesthood that you will read in this
booklet came out of the hearts and prayers of the authors
— out of the heart of Monsignor Dunne who has loved and
lived his priesthood to the fullest for sixty-five years — and out
of the many months his coauthor spent praying, meditating

and writing before the Blessed Sacrament. These prayers are meant for all to pray — priests, religious and laity — but they are written with the special purpose of providing insights into the life of a priest and into the mystery of the priesthood itself that will awaken and encourage in the laity a desire to pray for priests and for holy vocations.

As this booklet is about to be published, the Holy Father, Pope Benedict XVI, has announced a special 'Year for Priests', emphasizing the centrality of Christ in the "…priestly ministry, without which there would be no Eucharist, no mission, not even the Church." The Holy Father, in his message for the World Day of Prayer for Vocations in May, 2009, also stressed that "…prayer for vocations should be continuous and trusting."

Dear readers, just as we believe that there is no more fruitful investment in the life of the Church than prayer for Her priests, so we believe that one of the many fruits of a holy priesthood is vocations. We pray that this booklet will be an aid to those who will answer the Holy Father's call to prayer — throughout the year and beyond.

PART I

EXPOSITION OF THE BLESSED SACRAMENT (Kneel)

"O Salutaris Hostia"

O Salutaris Hostia

Quae coeli pandis ostium:

Bella premunt hostilia,

Da robur, fer auxilium.

Uni trinoque Domino,

Sit sempiterna gloria,

Qui vitam sine termino

Nobis donet in patria.
              Amen.

"O Saving Victim"

O saving Victim, opening wide

The gate of heav'n to man below.

Our foes press on from ev'ry side;

Thine aid supply; Thy strength bestow.

To Thy great name be endless praise,

Immortal Godhead, One in Three,

Oh, grant us endless length of days,

In our true native land with Thee.
              Amen.

Recite the following prayers:

O Sacrament Most Holy, O Sacrament Divine,
All praise and all thanksgiving be every moment Thine!
(*3 times*)

PRAYERS FOR THE HOLY FATHER

Prayers for the Holy Father, Pope (N.), for his health, his safety
and his intentions — **Our Father, Hail Mary, Glory Be**

SERRA PRAYER FOR VOCATIONS

O God Who wills not the death of a sinner, but rather that
he be converted and live, grant we beseech You, through the
intercession of the Blessed Mary, ever Virgin, Saint Joseph,
Her spouse, Blessed Junipero Serra and all the saints an
increase of laborers for Your Church, fellow laborers with
Christ to spend and consume themselves for souls, through
the same Jesus Christ, Your Son, Who lives and reigns with
You, in the unity of the Holy Spirit, God forever and ever.
                                                    Amen.

OPENING PRAYER FOR PRIESTS

All: O Most Holy Trinity,
Father, Son, and Holy Spirit,
we adore You and we love You with all our hearts.
We come before You,
humbly and prayerfully,
to intercede for all Your holy priesthood.
(We lift up in a special way all the priests who reside in our diocese.)

Father, we give You thanks with grateful hearts for the faithful
witness of so many priest-sons. Bless and protect them,
Father, hold them and shelter them in the palm of Your Hand.

Jesus, Eternal High Priest,
we lift up to You those priests who suffer and struggle,
those who are heavy-burdened,
and those who have lost their way.
Bless and heal them, Jesus,
You Who have said,
"Come to Me all you who find life burdensome…
  and I will give you rest."

Holy Spirit, Eternal Love of the Father and the Son,
pour out Your Love, Your Gifts, and Your Graces on every
priest of God. Strengthen them, Holy Spirit, fill them and
assure them of our love.

O Mary, Mother of Jesus,
Queen and Mother of all priests,
intercede for these special sons of Yours.
Hold them in Your Immaculate Heart, cradle them in Your arms,
protect them from every evil bent against them,
teach them to love, and lead them at last
into the arms of Your Son in Heaven.

                                 Amen.

Leader: Eucharistic Heart of Jesus, Model of the Priestly Heart,

All: **Have mercy on all priests.**

READING FROM SCRIPTURE (Stand)

(The Gospel of the day or the Gospel for the coming Sunday may be used or the leader may choose from the Scripture readings given in Appendix A)

PAUSE FOR SILENT REFLECTION (Sit)

(A short homily/meditation may be given if a priest/deacon is present)

Leader: Come, Holy Spirit, fill the hearts of Thy faithful.

All: **Enkindle in us the fire of Thy Love.**

Leader: Send forth Thy Spirit, and they shall be created,

All: **And Thou shalt renew the face of the earth.**

Leader: Let us pray:

All: **O God, Who by the light of the Holy Spirit, did instruct the hearts of the faithful, grant that by that same Holy Spirit, we may be truly wise and ever rejoice in His consolation through Christ our Lord. Amen.**

Leader: Thou, O Lord, will open my lips.

All: **And my tongue shall announce Thy praise.**

Leader: O God, come to my assistance.

All: **Lord, make haste to help me.**

Leader: Glory to the Father and to the Son and to the Holy Spirit.

All: **As it was in the beginning is now and ever shall be, world without end.** **Amen.**

THE HOLY ROSARY

The Apostles' Creed

All: I believe in God, the Father Almighty, Creator
of Heaven and earth; and in Jesus Christ,
His only Son, our Lord, Who was conceived
by the Holy Spirit, born of the Virgin Mary,
suffered under Pontius Pilate, was crucified, died,
and was buried.

He descended into hell. On the third day
He arose again from the dead; He ascended into
Heaven, and is seated at the right hand of God,
the Father Almighty; from thence He shall come
to judge the living and the dead.

I believe in the Holy Spirit, the Holy Catholic Church,
the Communion of Saints, the forgiveness of sins,
the resurrection of the body, and life everlasting.

Amen.

Our Father, three Hail Marys, Glory Be

The Mysteries of the Rosary

Hail Holy Queen

All: Hail Holy Queen, Mother of Mercy, our life, our sweetness and our hope. To Thee do we cry, poor banished children of Eve. To Thee do we send up our sighs, mourning and weeping in this valley of tears. Turn then, most gracious Advocate, Thine eyes of mercy toward us, and after this, our exile, show unto us the Blessed Fruit of Thy womb, Jesus. O clement, O loving, O sweet Virgin Mary!

Leader: Pray for us O Holy Mother of God,

All: That we may be made worthy of the promises of Christ.

Leader: Let us pray.

All: O God Whose only begotten Son by His life, death, and resurrection has purchased for us the rewards of eternal life; grant we beseech Thee, that meditating on these mysteries of the Most Holy Rosary of the Blessed Virgin Mary, we may imitate what they contain and obtain what they promise through the same Christ our Lord.

Amen.

THE JOYFUL MYSTERIES

The Annunciation

The angel announces to Mary that She will conceive in Her womb and bear a Son Who will be called Son of the Most High. Mary's "Yes", Her great *fiat*, reverberates for all time and eternity — and the Word is made flesh — God becomes Man and dwells among us.

We pray that all young men who are being called by God to the priesthood will give their consent to the Will of God.

We pray that all priests will truly love and cherish their participation in the Sacred Priesthood, conscious that their *fiat*, like Mary's, resounds through all time and eternity: "You are a priest forever according to the order of Melchizedek." [1]

The Visitation

Mary, with the Infant Jesus in Her Womb, travels in haste to the home of Elizabeth. The infant John the Baptist in the womb of Elizabeth leaps for joy, and Elizabeth herself is filled with the Holy Spirit at the sound of Mary's voice and the presence of the Lord so near.

We pray that all priests might live and love to bring Jesus to others — that they might be the merciful, healing presence of Christ as they visit the sick, the elderly, the imprisoned and the dying.

We pray that all priests might work reverently and tirelessly to protect and defend all human life.

The Birth of Jesus

Mary gives birth to the Prince of Peace, the Light of the World, in the darkness and poverty of a stable in Bethlehem. Through Her, the Eternal Word of the Father comes as a little child to bring us the Father's message of love and forgiveness. This is the true gift of Christmas.

We pray that all priests will place their hope and trust in this message of the Father's love and forgiveness that they, too, may become as little children of God.

And we pray that as they live out this Christmas message in their own lives throughout the year, they will inspire in others the hope Christ came to bring us.

The Presentation

Mary and Joseph present Jesus in the Temple according to the Law of Moses. Simeon, a holy and devout man "awaiting the consolation of Israel" [2], takes the Child in his arms and blesses God, telling Mary that Her Son will be a "sign that will be contradicted" [3] and that Her own heart will be pierced.

We pray that all priests — "signs of contradiction" in the world today — might be messengers of God's love and peace and consolation to the whole world.

We pray that all priests might unite themselves to the Heart of Mary when their hearts, too, are pierced by the pain and suffering that is both around and within them.

The Finding of the Boy Jesus in the Temple

Mary and Joseph, after three days of anxious searching, find the Child Jesus sitting among the teachers in the Temple. He returns with Mary and Joseph to Nazareth and is obedient to them.

We pray that all priests may be found teaching the faith in word and action wherever they may be.

We pray that all priests might turn to Mary and Joseph with obedient and childlike trust in all their needs as Jesus surely did, and that, like Jesus, they may grow in wisdom and age and grace in the sight of God. [4]

1 Hebrews 7:17 (NAB)   2 Luke 2:25 (NAB)   3 Luke 2:34 (NAB)   4 Luke 2:52 (NAB)

THE LUMINOUS MYSTERIES

The Baptism of Jesus

The Son of God, in profound humility, approaches John the Baptist and descends into the waters of the Jordan to be baptized by him. The Beloved Son sanctifies for all time the waters of baptism "while the Spirit descends on Him to invest Him with the mission which He is to carry out." [5]

We pray that all priests, like Jesus, will humbly and lovingly accept the mission of their vocation to serve and suffer for the people of God.

We pray that every priest might be a voice in the spiritual wilderness of today's society, calling souls to repentance and inviting them to meet and recognize Jesus as John the Baptist did — "Behold, the Lamb of God, Who takes away the sin of the world." [6]

The Wedding Feast at Cana

Mary, with simplicity and genuine concern, says to Her Son, "They have no wine." [7] And with faith in Her Divine Son, She turns to the servants at the wedding and says, "… do whatever He tells you." [8] Jesus responds with the first of His public miracles — changing water into wine.

We pray that all priests, with loving simplicity, will follow Mary's counsel to "… do whatever He tells you." They, too, will see miracles.

We pray for all priests as they teach and prepare couples for the Sacrament of Marriage.

We pray that every priest will cherish his own spousal relationship with Holy Mother Church and live it out with sensitivity, chastity and love.

The Proclamation of the Kingdom of God and Call to Discipleship

Jesus came to reconcile mankind to the Father, ushering in this ministry of reconciliation with the first words of His public ministry, "… the Kingdom of God is at hand. Repent and believe in the Gospel." [9]

We pray that all priests will be gentle and compassionate ministers of the Sacrament of Reconciliation.

We pray that all priests throughout their lives of ministry will pray and study the Gospels with fervor, and that as they break open the Gospel message for the faithful each day, they will preach it with truth and boldness and live it with love.

The Transfiguration

Jesus takes Peter, James and John up the mountain where, in the presence of Moses and Elijah, He reveals to them His glory, thus strengthening their faith for the road to Calvary which lies ahead.

We pray that all priests can and will immerse themselves in prayer daily and experience in this the love and peace of God that strengthens them for their daily trials.

We pray that as each priest prays and listens to the voice of the Beloved Son, he will be transfigured into a more perfect image of the Love of Christ, his eyes ever on Jesus and the glory that follows a life lived in fidelity to Him.

The Institution of the Holy Eucharist

Jesus institutes the Eucharist and the ministerial priesthood at the Last Supper. These two — the Eucharist and the priesthood — can NEVER be separated.

The priest must find his happiness — his joy — in his oneness with Christ. This oneness realizes its fullest expression at the moment of Consecration at every Mass when the priest, *in persona Christi*, offers himself as both priest and victim for the salvation of souls.

We pray that every priest will believe in the True Presence of Jesus in the Holy Eucharist and will faithfully and reverently celebrate Mass each day, adoring the Lord Whom he holds in his hands and witnessing his love for Christ in the Most Blessed Sacrament.

We pray for priests preparing souls of all ages for their First Communion and for those priests preparing seminarians for the Sacrament of Holy Orders.

5 *Rosarium Virginis Mariae*, 21   6 *John 1:29 (NAB)*   7 *John 2:3 (NAB)*   8 *John 2:5 (NAB)*   9 *Mark 1:15 (NAB)*

THE SORROWFUL MYSTERIES

The Agony in the Garden

Jesus, in fervent prayer in the Garden of Gethsemane, sweats blood as He sees the suffering, torture and humiliation that awaits Him. He feels the weight of the sins of mankind and knows that His sacrifice will be a scandal to some, misunderstood and rejected by others. In the midst of this dark and bitter agony, Jesus surrenders — "Not My will, [Father,] but Thine, be done." [10]

It is the privilege and obligation of every priest everywhere to give his life for the sanctification and salvation of souls. We pray that all priests will surrender themselves into the hands of the Father each day, no matter what it costs.

We pray that every priest can place his trust fully in the Lord, especially in the midst of darkness, misunderstanding or humiliation — when his best efforts for the good of souls appear to be in vain.

The Scourging at the Pillar

Jesus is bound to a pillar and His Sacred Flesh is mercilessly scourged. His Precious Blood flows freely from His open wounds.

We pray that all priests will remain faithful to the discipline of celibacy and be diligent by their words and their example in promoting purity and chastity in all vocations.

We pray that every priest who, through weakness and neglect of his relationship with Christ, has fallen into sin, ignored or rejected the teachings of the Church, or abandoned his vocation, may repent and return to the merciful love of God.

The Crowning with Thorns

Jesus' Sacred Head is pierced deeply with a crown of thorns. Again, His Precious Blood flows freely for us. He is mocked and spat upon, but the "man of sorrows, despised and rejected, opens not his mouth." [11]

We pray that all priests will strive for and cherish the virtue of humility, shunning every show of pride and seeking always to carry out their duties with humble and sincere obedience, in the sure knowledge that the least assignment for the Kingdom is no less than the greatest when all is done for the love of God.

We pray that all priests, like Jesus, will look with kindly and fatherly eyes on the great and the small, the rich and the poor alike in their ministry.

The Carrying of the Cross

Jesus carries His heavy Cross up the hill of Calvary, falling again and again under the weight of our sins. He is exhausted, in terrible pain and surrounded by brutality.

We pray here especially for priests who, being falsely accused or having actually fallen in some way, must yet endure scorn, gossip and rejection rather than the love and prayer they need.

We pray that every priest, when he sees a fallen brother, will come to his aid with the fraternal charity and prayer he needs for support and healing.

The Crucifixion and Death of Jesus

Jesus came into the world to show us the way to the Father. Now, in His final hour, hanging in agony on the Cross, He reveals the depth of God's love and mercy by giving His life to redeem us from sin and death.

We pray for all priests as they administer the Anointing of the Sick and carry *Viaticum* to the dying.

For all priests who are now on their deathbed and those who will die this day, we ask for the grace of final perseverance. We pray, too, that through their union with Christ on the Cross, they may find the strength to forgive all who have offended them throughout their ministry.

And we pray for the souls of all priests in Purgatory.

10 Luke 22:42 (RSV)   11 Isaiah 53:3,7 (RSV)

THE GLORIOUS MYSTERIES

The Resurrection

Jesus Christ is Risen! We sing Alleluia!!

Here is the foundational truth of our faith. Jesus has broken the power of death, reconciled God and mankind, and opened for all the gates of Heaven.

We pray that all priests who suffer through painful trials will unite themselves to the suffering Christ that they may come to know with Him the light and joy of the Resurrection.

We pray that all priests will celebrate the Resurrection with Easter joy every Sunday.

The Ascension

If the truth of the Resurrection is the foundation of our faith, the Ascension is surely the basis for our hope.

Jesus came to show a lost and fallen humanity the way to the Father. Now, as He returns to the Father, He takes our restored humanity with Him, leaving His apostles with the instructions to carry the Gospel into the whole world, making disciples of all the nations and baptizing in the name of the Father and of the Son and of the Holy Spirit.[12] To this very day, every priest is ordained and sent for this same purpose.

We pray for all priests as they open the doors of salvation to countless souls through the saving waters of Baptism.

We pray for the safety and protection of all priests, especially missionary priests who carry the Gospel message into dangerous and sometimes violent areas of the world.

We lift up, in a special way, those priests who will shed their blood for the Gospel of Jesus Christ.

The Descent of the Holy Spirit

The Holy Spirit descends in tongues of fire on the apostles, filling them with the Love of God, sanctifying them and empowering them to go forth to announce and explain the

Word of God with authority.[13] In a similar way, the Holy Spirit descends on every priest at his ordination to remain with him for all time in his ministry to the people of God.

We pray for all priests as they prepare souls for a new infilling of the Holy Spirit at Confirmation.

We pray that every priest might prayerfully beg for the gifts of the Holy Spirit and seek opportunities to gather with his brother priests and the faithful to pray, to praise God, and to call forth the gifts of the Holy Spirit to help build up the Body of Christ.

The Assumption

Mary is assumed body and soul into Heaven.

The language of true love — the proof of true love — is sacrifice. Like Her crucified Son Who sacrificed all to redeem us, Mary has sacrificed Her entire life to God. And when, at the foot of the Cross, Jesus said to Her, "Woman, behold, Your son," [14] She took into Her heart not just John, but all of humanity and, in a special way, every priest for all time and eternity.

We pray that every priest will cherish deeply his filial relationship with Mary, that he will love Her, turn to Her in all his needs, spread devotion to Her and at last commend himself into Her maternal arms at the hour of his death.

The Coronation

Mary, most humble of all God's children, is crowned Queen. She is exalted forever over every creature in the Heavens above and on earth below!

As Queen and Mother of all priests, Mary remains at the side of each of Her sons throughout his life of ministry, guiding, inspiring and exhorting him and interceding for him before the Throne of God.

We pray for the holiness and fidelity of every priest from the day of his ordination to the day he, too, enters eternity where he may take his place with Mary and the entire Communion of Saints to experience forever the incomprehensible Love of God. "*Deus meus et omnia* … my God and my all!"

12 Matthew 28:19 (NAB)   13 Directory on the Ministry and Life of Priests, 9   14 John 19:26 (NAB)

GENERAL INTERCESSIONS FOR PRIESTS

(All of the following intercessions may be used or the leader may select from the list)

Leader: For the Holy Father, Pope (N.), protect him, Lord, and fill him with love and courage. Let him be a sign to the whole world that he is truly the Vicar of Christ, the successor of Peter, we pray to the Lord …

All: **Lord hear our prayer.**

Leader: For all shepherds of the Church, that they may have hearts after the Heart of the Good Shepherd, always obedient to the Holy Father and all bishops in communion with him, we pray to the Lord …

All: **Lord hear our prayer.**

Leader: For all priests, that they may be filled with the gifts of the Holy Spirit as they listen, preach and minister to the people of God, we pray to the Lord …

All: **Lord hear our prayer.**

Leader: For all priests, that they may always teach, defend and remain faithful to the truths of the Catholic Church, and be willing to speak up or stand their ground when these truths are challenged, we pray to the Lord …

All: **Lord hear our prayer.**

Leader: That all priests, as they celebrate Mass, might approach the altar with great love for Christ and a deep sense of reverence for the Sacred Mysteries they are about to enter into, we pray to the Lord …

All: **Lord hear our prayer.**

Leader: That all priests, wherever they may be, will always be enlightened, inspired and compassionate ministers of the Sacraments, we pray to the Lord …

All: **Lord hear our prayer.**

Leader: That all priests responsible for teaching in our schools may be gifted to teach with clarity and conviction as they open the truths of the faith to the young, we pray to the Lord …

All: **Lord hear our prayer.**

Leader: That all priests will make every effort to pray and study the Scriptures and grow in their knowledge and understanding of the teachings of the Church so as to be effective preachers of the Gospel, we pray to the Lord …

All: **Lord hear our prayer.**

Leader: For all priests who guide and direct souls, especially those priests responsible for directing the souls of their brother priests, that they may be filled with the gifts of the Holy Spirit, especially wisdom and prudence, and be enlightened and equipped for this ministry, we pray to the Lord …

All: **Lord hear our prayer.**

Leader: For all priests who have grown old in the service of the Lord and His Church, that they may be lovingly sustained and cared for in all their needs, we pray to the Lord …

All: **Lord hear our prayer.**

Leader: For all priests, that they may always know the love, support, and encouragement of their brother priests, especially in their hour of need, we pray to the Lord …

All: **Lord hear our prayer.**

Leader: For all priests, that they may be faithful to a life of prayer and that they may experience in their prayer the love of God which surpasses all understanding, we pray to the Lord …

All: **Lord hear our prayer.**

Leader: That all priests will always advocate, protect and defend the sanctity of all human life, we pray to the Lord …

All: **Lord hear our prayer.**

Leader: That all priests will teach, promote and help make available to the faithful the approved devotions of the Church, we pray to the Lord …

All: **Lord hear our prayer.**

Leader: That all priests will defend and remain faithful to the discipline of celibacy, especially in a world that does not value this sacrifice, we pray to the Lord …

All: **Lord hear our prayer.**

For the fidelity and sanctity of every priest, that
through his life of prayer and oneness with Christ, his
example may draw the faithful in his care to a deeper
relationship with Christ, we pray to the Lord …

All: **Lord hear our prayer.**

(Optional) **Pause to add own intentions for priests**

All: **Our Father who art in Heaven hallowed be
Thy name; Thy Kingdom come, Thy will be done,
on earth as it is in Heaven. Give us this day our daily
bread and forgive us our trespasses as we forgive
those who trespass against us. And lead us not into
temptation, but deliver us from evil.**

Leader: Let us pray:

All: **O my Jesus, I beg You on behalf of the whole Church:
Grant it love and the light of Your Spirit, and give power
to the words of priests so that hardened hearts might
be brought to repentance and return to You, O Lord.**

**Lord, give us holy priests; You Yourself maintain them
in holiness. O Divine and Great High Priest, may the
power of Your Mercy accompany them everywhere and
protect them from the devil's traps and snares which
are continually being set for the souls of priests. May
the power of Your Mercy, O Lord, shatter and bring to
naught all that might tarnish the sanctity of priests,
for You can do all things.**[15]   **Amen.**

15 Divine Mercy in My Soul, (Diary, #1052)

PAUSE FOR SILENT REFLECTION (Sit)

CONCLUDING PRAYERS (Kneel)

Benediction Hymn

"Tantum Ergo"	**Down in Adoration Falling**
Tantum ergo Sacramentum,	Down in adoration falling,
Veneremur cernui:	This great Sacrament we hail;
Et antiquum documentum	Over ancient forms of worship
Novo cedat ritui:	Newer rites of grace prevail;
Praestet fides supplementum	Faith tells us that Christ is present
Sensuum defectui.	When our human senses fail.
Genitori, Genitoque	To the Everlasting Father,
Laus et jubilatio,	And the Son who made us free,
Salus, honor, virtus quoque,	And the Spirit, God proceeding
Sit et benedictio:	From Them each eternally.
Procedenti ab utroque	Be salvation, honor, blessing,
Compar sit laudatio.	Might and endless majesty.

Leader: You have given them bread from Heaven.

All: **Having all sweetness within it.**

Leader: Let us pray: Lord Jesus Christ, You gave us the
Eucharist as the memorial of Your suffering and death.
May our worship of this Sacrament of Your Body and
Blood help us to experience the salvation You won for
us and the peace of the Kingdom where You live with the
Father and the Holy Spirit, one God, for ever and ever.

BENEDICTION

*A blessing with the monstrance may be given
if there is a priest or deacon present.*

"The Divine Praises"

Blessed be God.

Blessed be His Holy Name.

Blessed be Jesus Christ, true God and true Man.

Blessed be the Name of Jesus.

Blessed be His Most Sacred Heart.

Blessed be His Most Precious Blood.

Blessed be Jesus in the Most Holy Sacrament
of the Altar.

Blessed be the Holy Spirit, the Paraclete.

Blessed be the Great Mother of God,
Mary Most Holy.

Blessed be Her Holy
and Immaculate Conception.

Blessed be Her Glorious Assumption.

Blessed be the Name of Mary,
Virgin and Mother.

Blessed be St. Joseph,
Her most chaste spouse.

Blessed be God in His Angels
and in His Saints.

"O Sacrament Most Holy"

O Sacrament Most Holy,

O Sacrament Divine,

All praise and all thanksgiving

be every moment Thine!

(3 times)

"Holy God, We Praise Thy Name"

Holy God, we praise Thy Name;

Lord of all, we bow before Thee.

All on earth Thy scepter claim;

All in Heaven above adore Thee.

Infinite Thy vast domain,

Everlasting is Thy reign.

(repeat)

Hark! The loud celestial hymn,

Angel choirs above are raising.

Cherubim and Seraphim

In unceasing chorus praising,

Fill the Heavens with sweet accord

Holy, holy, holy Lord.

(repeat)

PART II

This format is suitable for prayer before the reposed
Blessed Sacrament, in homes, meeting places and for private prayer.
Other devotional prayers may be added if desired.

Prayer to the Holy Spirit

Leader: Come, Holy Spirit, fill the hearts of Thy faithful.

All: **Enkindle in us the fire of Your love.**

Leader: Send forth Your Spirit, and they shall be created,

All: **And Thou shalt renew the face of the earth.**

Leader: Let us pray:

All: **O God, Who by the light of the Holy Spirit, did instruct the hearts of the faithful, grant that by that same Holy Spirit, we may be truly wise and ever rejoice in His consolation through Christ our Lord.**

Amen.

Prayers for the Holy Father

Prayers for the Holy Father, Pope (N.), for his health, his safety and his intentions — **Our Father, Hail Mary, Glory Be**

Serra Prayer for Vocations

O God Who wills not the death of a sinner, but rather that he be converted and live, grant we beseech You, through the intercession of the Blessed Mary, ever Virgin, Saint Joseph, Her spouse, Blessed Junipero Serra and all the saints an increase of laborers for Your Church, fellow laborers with Christ to spend and consume themselves for souls, through the same Jesus Christ, Your Son, Who lives and reigns with You, in the unity of the Holy Spirit, God forever and ever.

Amen.

OPENING PRAYER FOR PRIESTS

All: O Most Holy Trinity,
Father, Son, and Holy Spirit,
we adore You and we love You with all our hearts.
We come before You,
humbly and prayerfully,
to intercede for all Your holy priesthood.
(We lift up in a special way all the priests who reside in our diocese.)

Father, we give You thanks with grateful hearts for the faithful
witness of so many priest-sons. Bless and protect them,
Father, hold them and shelter them in the palm of Your Hand.

Jesus, Eternal High Priest,
we lift up to You those priests who suffer and struggle,
those who are heavy-burdened,
and those who have lost their way.
Bless and heal them, Jesus,
You Who have said,
"Come to Me all you who find life burdensome…
  and I will give you rest."

Holy Spirit, Eternal Love of the Father and the Son,
pour out Your Love, Your Gifts, and Your Graces on every
priest of God. Strengthen them, Holy Spirit, fill them and
assure them of our love.

O Mary, Mother of Jesus,
Queen and Mother of all priests,
intercede for these special sons of Yours.
Hold them in Your Immaculate Heart, cradle them in Your arms,
protect them from every evil bent against them,
teach them to love, and lead them at last
into the arms of Your Son in Heaven.

                                        Amen.

Leader: Eucharistic Heart of Jesus, Model of the Priestly Heart,

All: **Have Mercy on all priests.**

(Optional) **Reading from Scripture**

(See Appendix A for suggested Scripture readings)

Pause for Silent Reflection

THE HOLY ROSARY

The Apostles' Creed

All: I believe in God, the Father Almighty, Creator
of Heaven and earth; and in Jesus Christ,
His only Son, our Lord, Who was conceived
by the Holy Spirit, born of the Virgin Mary,
suffered under Pontius Pilate, was crucified, died,
and was buried.

He descended into hell. On the third day
He arose again from the dead; He ascended into
Heaven, and is seated at the right hand of God,
the Father Almighty; from thence He shall come
to judge the living and the dead.

I believe in the Holy Spirit, the Holy Catholic Church,
the Communion of Saints, the forgiveness of sins,
the resurrection of the body, and life everlasting.

Amen.

Our Father, three Hail Marys, Glory Be

The Mysteries of the Rosary

Hail Holy Queen

All: Hail Holy Queen, Mother of Mercy, our life, our sweetness and our hope. To Thee do we cry, poor banished children of Eve. To Thee do we send up our sighs, mourning and weeping in this valley of tears. Turn then, most gracious Advocate, Thine eyes of mercy toward us, and after this, our exile, show unto us the Blessed Fruit of Thy womb, Jesus. O clement, O loving, O sweet Virgin Mary!

Leader: Pray for us O Holy Mother of God,

All: That we may be made worthy of the promises of Christ.

Leader: Let us pray.

All: O God Whose only begotten Son by His life, death, and resurrection has purchased for us the rewards of eternal life; grant we beseech Thee, that meditating on these mysteries of the Most Holy Rosary of the Blessed Virgin Mary, we may imitate what they contain and obtain what they promise through the same Christ our Lord.

Amen.

THE JOYFUL MYSTERIES

The Annunciation

The angel announces to Mary that She will conceive in Her womb and bear a Son Who will be called Son of the Most High. Mary's "Yes", Her great *fiat*, reverberates for all time and eternity — and the Word is made flesh — God becomes Man and dwells among us.

We pray that all young men who are being called by God to the priesthood will give their consent to the Will of God.

We pray that all priests will truly love and cherish their participation in the Sacred Priesthood, conscious that their *fiat*, like Mary's, resounds through all time and eternity: "You are a priest forever according to the order of Melchizedek." [1]

The Visitation

Mary, with the Infant Jesus in Her Womb, travels in haste to the home of Elizabeth. The infant John the Baptist in the womb of Elizabeth leaps for joy, and Elizabeth herself is filled with the Holy Spirit at the sound of Mary's voice and the presence of the Lord so near.

We pray that all priests might live and love to bring Jesus to others — that they might be the merciful, healing presence of Christ as they visit the sick, the elderly, the imprisoned and the dying.

We pray that all priests might work reverently and tirelessly to protect and defend all human life.

The Birth of Jesus

Mary gives birth to the Prince of Peace, the Light of the World, in the darkness and poverty of a stable in Bethlehem. Through Her, the Eternal Word of the Father comes as a little child to bring us the Father's message of love and forgiveness. This is the true gift of Christmas.

We pray that all priests will place their hope and trust in this message of the Father's love and forgiveness that they, too, may become as little children of God.

And we pray that as they live out this Christmas message in their own lives throughout the year, they will inspire in others the hope Christ came to bring us.

The Presentation

Mary and Joseph present Jesus in the Temple according to the Law of Moses. Simeon, a holy and devout man "awaiting the consolation of Israel" [2], takes the Child in his arms and blesses God, telling Mary that Her Son will be a "sign that will be contradicted" [3] and that Her own heart will be pierced.

We pray that all priests — "signs of contradiction" in the world today — might be messengers of God's love and peace and consolation to the whole world.

We pray that all priests might unite themselves to the Heart of Mary when their hearts, too, are pierced by the pain and suffering that is both around and within them.

The Finding of the Boy Jesus in the Temple

Mary and Joseph, after three days of anxious searching, find the Child Jesus sitting among the teachers in the Temple. He returns with Mary and Joseph to Nazareth and is obedient to them.

We pray that all priests may be found teaching the faith in word and action wherever they may be.

We pray that all priests might turn to Mary and Joseph with obedient and childlike trust in all their needs as Jesus surely did, and that, like Jesus, they may grow in wisdom and age and grace in the sight of God.[4]

1 Hebrews 7:17 (NAB)   2 Luke 2:25 (NAB)   3 Luke 2:34 (NAB)   4 Luke 2:52 (NAB)

THE LUMINOUS MYSTERIES

The Baptism of Jesus

The Son of God, in profound humility, approaches John the Baptist and descends into the waters of the Jordan to be baptized by him. The Beloved Son sanctifies for all time the waters of baptism "while the Spirit descends on Him to invest Him with the mission which He is to carry out." [5]

We pray that all priests, like Jesus, will humbly and lovingly accept the mission of their vocation to serve and suffer for the people of God.

We pray that every priest might be a voice in the spiritual wilderness of today's society, calling souls to repentance and inviting them to meet and recognize Jesus as John the Baptist did — "Behold, the Lamb of God, Who takes away the sin of the world." [6]

The Wedding Feast at Cana

Mary, with simplicity and genuine concern, says to Her Son, "They have no wine."[7] And with faith in Her Divine Son, She turns to the servants at the wedding and says, "… do whatever He tells you."[8] Jesus responds with the first of His public miracles — changing water into wine.

We pray that all priests, with loving simplicity, will follow Mary's counsel to "… do whatever He tells you." They, too, will see miracles.

We pray for all priests as they teach and prepare couples for the Sacrament of Marriage.

We pray that every priest will cherish his own spousal relationship with Holy Mother Church and live it out with sensitivity, chastity and love.

The Proclamation of the Kingdom of God and Call to Discipleship

Jesus came to reconcile mankind to the Father, ushering in this ministry of reconciliation with the first words of His public ministry, "… the Kingdom of God is at hand. Repent and believe in the Gospel." [9]

We pray that all priests will be gentle and compassionate ministers of the Sacrament of Reconciliation.

We pray that all priests throughout their lives of ministry will pray and study the Gospels with fervor, and that as they break open the Gospel message for the faithful each day, they will preach it with truth and boldness and live it with love.

The Transfiguration

Jesus takes Peter, James and John up the mountain where, in the presence of Moses and Elijah, He reveals to them His glory, thus strengthening their faith for the road to Calvary which lies ahead.

We pray that all priests can and will immerse themselves in prayer daily and experience in this the love and peace of God that strengthens them for their daily trials.

We pray that as each priest prays and listens to the voice of the Beloved Son, he will be transfigured into a more perfect image of the Love of Christ, his eyes ever on Jesus and the glory that follows a life lived in fidelity to Him.

The Institution of the Holy Eucharist

Jesus institutes the Eucharist and the ministerial priesthood at the Last Supper. These two — the Eucharist and the priesthood — can NEVER be separated.

The priest must find his happiness — his joy — in his oneness with Christ. This oneness realizes its fullest expression at the moment of Consecration at every Mass when the priest, *in persona Christi*, offers himself as both priest and victim for the salvation of souls.

We pray that every priest will believe in the True Presence of Jesus in the Holy Eucharist and will faithfully and reverently celebrate Mass each day, adoring the Lord Whom he holds in his hands and witnessing his love for Christ in the Most Blessed Sacrament.

We pray for priests preparing souls of all ages for their First Communion and for those priests preparing seminarians for the Sacrament of Holy Orders.

5 Rosarium Virginis Mariae, 21   *6 John 1:29 (NAB)*   *7 John 2:3 (NAB)*   *8 John 2:5 (NAB)*   *9 Mark 1:15 (NAB)*

THE SORROWFUL MYSTERIES

The Agony in the Garden

Jesus, in fervent prayer in the Garden of Gethsemane, sweats blood as He sees the suffering, torture and humiliation that awaits Him. He feels the weight of the sins of mankind and knows that His sacrifice will be a scandal to some, misunderstood and rejected by others. In the midst of this dark and bitter agony, Jesus surrenders — "Not My will, [Father,] but Thine, be done." [10]

It is the privilege and obligation of every priest everywhere to give his life for the sanctification and salvation of souls. We pray that all priests will surrender themselves into the hands of the Father each day, no matter what it costs.

We pray that every priest can place his trust fully in the Lord, especially in the midst of darkness, misunderstanding or humiliation — when his best efforts for the good of souls appear to be in vain.

The Scourging at the Pillar

Jesus is bound to a pillar and His Sacred Flesh is mercilessly scourged. His Precious Blood flows freely from His open wounds.

We pray that all priests will remain faithful to the discipline of celibacy and be diligent by their words and their example in promoting purity and chastity in all vocations.

We pray that every priest who, through weakness and neglect of his relationship with Christ, has fallen into sin, ignored or rejected the teachings of the Church, or abandoned his vocation, may repent and return to the merciful love of God.

The Crowning with Thorns

Jesus' Sacred Head is pierced deeply with a crown of thorns. Again, His Precious Blood flows freely for us. He is mocked and spat upon, but the "man of sorrows, despised and rejected, opens not his mouth." [11]

We pray that all priests will strive for and cherish the virtue of humility, shunning every show of pride and seeking always to carry out their duties with humble and sincere obedience, in the sure knowledge that the least assignment for the Kingdom is no less than the greatest when all is done for the love of God.

We pray that all priests, like Jesus, will look with kindly and fatherly eyes on the great and the small, the rich and the poor alike in their ministry.

The Carrying of the Cross

Jesus carries His heavy Cross up the hill of Calvary, falling again and again under the weight of our sins. He is exhausted, in terrible pain and surrounded by brutality.

We pray here especially for priests who, being falsely accused or having actually fallen in some way, must yet endure scorn, gossip and rejection rather than the love and prayer they need.

We pray that every priest, when he sees a fallen brother, will come to his aid with the fraternal charity and prayer he needs for support and healing.

The Crucifixion and Death of Jesus

Jesus came into the world to show us the way to the Father. Now, in His final hour, hanging in agony on the Cross, He reveals the depth of God's love and mercy by giving His life to redeem us from sin and death.

We pray for all priests as they administer the Anointing of the Sick and carry *Viaticum* to the dying.

For all priests who are now on their deathbed and those who will die this day, we ask for the grace of final perseverance. We pray, too, that through their union with Christ on the Cross, they may find the strength to forgive all who have offended them throughout their ministry.

And we pray for the souls of all priests in Purgatory.

THE GLORIOUS MYSTERIES

The Resurrection

Jesus Christ is Risen! We sing Alleluia!!

Here is the foundational truth of our faith. Jesus has broken the power of death, reconciled God and mankind, and opened for all the gates of Heaven.

We pray that all priests who suffer through painful trials will unite themselves to the suffering Christ that they may come to know with Him the light and joy of the Resurrection.

We pray that all priests will celebrate the Resurrection with Easter joy every Sunday.

The Ascension

If the truth of the Resurrection is the foundation of our faith, the Ascension is surely the basis for our hope.

Jesus came to show a lost and fallen humanity the way to the Father. Now, as He returns to the Father, He takes our restored humanity with Him, leaving His apostles with the instructions to carry the Gospel into the whole world, making disciples of all the nations and baptizing in the name of the Father and of the Son and of the Holy Spirit.[12] To this very day, every priest is ordained and sent for this same purpose.

We pray for all priests as they open the doors of salvation to countless souls through the saving waters of Baptism.

We pray for the safety and protection of all priests, especially missionary priests who carry the Gospel message into dangerous and sometimes violent areas of the world.

We lift up, in a special way, those priests who will shed their blood for the Gospel of Jesus Christ.

The Descent of the Holy Spirit

The Holy Spirit descends in tongues of fire on the apostles, filling them with the Love of God, sanctifying them and empowering them to go forth to announce and explain the

Word of God with authority.[13] In a similar way, the Holy Spirit descends on every priest at his ordination to remain with him for all time in his ministry to the people of God.

We pray for all priests as they prepare souls for a new infilling of the Holy Spirit at Confirmation.

We pray that every priest might prayerfully beg for the gifts of the Holy Spirit and seek opportunities to gather with his brother priests and the faithful to pray, to praise God, and to call forth the gifts of the Holy Spirit to help build up the Body of Christ.

The Assumption

Mary is assumed body and soul into Heaven.

The language of true love — the proof of true love — is sacrifice. Like Her crucified Son Who sacrificed all to redeem us, Mary has sacrificed Her entire life to God. And when, at the foot of the Cross, Jesus said to Her, "Woman, behold, Your son," [14] She took into Her heart not just John, but all of humanity and, in a special way, every priest for all time and eternity.

We pray that every priest will cherish deeply his filial relationship with Mary, that he will love Her, turn to Her in all his needs, spread devotion to Her and at last commend himself into Her maternal arms at the hour of his death.

The Coronation

Mary, most humble of all God's children, is crowned Queen. She is exalted forever over every creature in the Heavens above and on earth below!

As Queen and Mother of all priests, Mary remains at the side of each of Her sons throughout his life of ministry, guiding, inspiring and exhorting him and interceding for him before the Throne of God.

We pray for the holiness and fidelity of every priest from the day of his ordination to the day he, too, enters eternity where he may take his place with Mary and the entire Communion of Saints to experience forever the incomprehensible Love of God. "*Deus meus et omnia* … my God and my all!"

---

12 Matthew 28:19 (NAB)   13 Directory on the Ministry and Life of Priests, 9   14 John 19:26 (NAB)

GENERAL INTERCESSIONS FOR PRIESTS

(All of the following intercessions may be used or the leader may select from the list)

Leader: For the Holy Father, Pope (N.), protect him, Lord, and fill him with love and courage. Let him be a sign to the whole world that he is truly the Vicar of Christ, the successor of Peter, we pray to the Lord …

All: **Lord hear our prayer.**

Leader: For all shepherds of the Church, that they may have hearts after the Heart of the Good Shepherd, always obedient to the Holy Father and all bishops in communion with him, we pray to the Lord …

All: **Lord hear our prayer.**

Leader: For all priests, that they may be filled with the gifts of the Holy Spirit as they listen, preach and minister to the people of God, we pray to the Lord …

All: **Lord hear our prayer.**

Leader: For all priests, that they may always teach, defend and remain faithful to the truths of the Catholic Church, and be willing to speak up or stand their ground when these truths are challenged, we pray to the Lord …

All: **Lord hear our prayer.**

Leader: That all priests, as they celebrate Mass, might approach the altar with great love for Christ and a deep sense of reverence for the Sacred Mysteries they are about to enter into, we pray to the Lord …

All: **Lord hear our prayer.**

Leader: That all priests, wherever they may be, will always be enlightened, inspired and compassionate ministers of the Sacraments, we pray to the Lord …

All: **Lord hear our prayer.**

Leader: That all priests responsible for teaching in our schools may be gifted to teach with clarity and conviction as they open the truths of the faith to the young, we pray to the Lord …

All: **Lord hear our prayer.**

Leader: That all priests will make every effort to pray and study the Scriptures and grow in their knowledge and understanding of the teachings of the Church so as to be effective preachers of the Gospel, we pray to the Lord …

All: **Lord hear our prayer.**

Leader: For all priests who guide and direct souls, especially those priests responsible for directing the souls of their brother priests, that they may be filled with the gifts of the Holy Spirit, especially wisdom and prudence, and be enlightened and equipped for this ministry, we pray to the Lord …

All: **Lord hear our prayer.**

Leader: For all priests who have grown old in the service of the Lord and His Church, that they may be lovingly sustained and cared for in all their needs, we pray to the Lord …

All: **Lord hear our prayer.**

Leader: For all priests, that they may always know the love, support, and encouragement of their brother priests, especially in their hour of need, we pray to the Lord …

All: **Lord hear our prayer.**

Leader: For all priests, that they may be faithful to a life of prayer and that they may experience in their prayer the love of God which surpasses all understanding, we pray to the Lord …

All: **Lord hear our prayer.**

Leader: That all priests will always advocate, protect and defend the sanctity of all human life, we pray to the Lord …

All: **Lord hear our prayer.**

Leader: That all priests will teach, promote and help make available to the faithful the approved devotions of the Church, we pray to the Lord …

All: **Lord hear our prayer.**

Leader: That all priests will defend and remain faithful to the discipline of celibacy, especially in a world that does not value this sacrifice, we pray to the Lord …

All: **Lord hear our prayer.**

For the fidelity and sanctity of every priest, that
through his life of prayer and oneness with Christ, his
example may draw the faithful in his care to a deeper
relationship with Christ, we pray to the Lord …

All: **Lord hear our prayer.**

(Optional) **Pause to add own intentions for priests**

All: **Our Father who art in Heaven hallowed be
Thy name; Thy Kingdom come, Thy will be done,
on earth as it is in Heaven. Give us this day our daily
bread and forgive us our trespasses as we forgive
those who trespass against us. And lead us not into
temptation, but deliver us from evil.**

Leader: Let us pray:

All: **O my Jesus, I beg You on behalf of the whole Church:
Grant it love and the light of Your Spirit, and give power
to the words of priests so that hardened hearts might
be brought to repentance and return to You, O Lord.**

**Lord, give us holy priests; You Yourself maintain them
in holiness. O Divine and Great High Priest, may the
power of Your Mercy accompany them everywhere and
protect them from the devil's traps and snares which
are continually being set for the souls of priests. May
the power of Your Mercy, O Lord, shatter and bring to
naught all that might tarnish the sanctity of priests,
for You can do all things.**[15]   **Amen.**

15 *Divine Mercy in My Soul, (Diary, #1052)*

PART III

**THE STATIONS OF THE CROSS
WITH MEDITATIONS ON THE PRIESTHOOD**

Introduction

It is not possible for any lay person, male or female, to grasp or comprehend fully the sublime vocation to the Sacred Priesthood of Jesus Christ or what it means to live out this calling.

Each of us, in a very real sense, is called to live our lives walking with Jesus up the hill of Calvary. But it is a deep reality — a deep and sacred reality — that those ordained to the priesthood will, *in persona Christi*, lay down their lives for others.

We, as laity, can never enter fully into the mystery of the life of a priest, but we might, on occasion, discover a "window" through which we catch a glimpse or gain a little deeper understanding of his life as he lives it on the road to Calvary with Jesus.

In writing these short meditations on the priesthood for the Stations of the Cross, we hope to offer you a "window" such as this to look through. As you make the Stations with these meditations, please consider offering them for the sanctification of all priests and their fidelity to their vocation.

The Way of the Cross

The Sign of the Cross (+)

Leader: In the Name of the Father, and of the Son,
and of the Holy Spirit.

All: **Amen.**

Opening Prayer

All: **Lord Jesus Christ, You entrusted Your Church to the apostles, Your first priests, and willed that they and those who would follow after them should take up their Cross and follow You. To this day, this sacrificial nature of Your Holy Priesthood remains unchanged.**

Grant, O Lord, that, through the merits of these prayers and meditations on Your passion and death, Your priests may come to love You more deeply and follow You more faithfully.

We ask this through the Sorrowful and Immaculate Heart of Mary, the first to make this Way of the Cross with You.

Amen.

THE LORD JESUS IS CONDEMNED TO DEATH

I

FIRST STATION — Jesus is Condemned to Death

Leader: We adore You, O Christ, and we praise You;

All: **Because by Your Holy Cross,
You have redeemed the world.**

Jesus, in God's plan of salvation, offers His life
on the Cross for us.

Here is the priest at his ordination. It is a wondrous and
happy day — yet, the priest, now *alter Christus*, that is,
another Christ, will offer his life for the sanctification
and salvation of souls.

Leader: Lord Jesus Crucified,
All: **Have mercy on all priests.**

THE LORD JESUS TAKES THE HEAVY CROSS ON HIMSELF
II

SECOND STATION – Jesus Accepts His Cross

Leader: We adore You, O Christ, and we praise You;

All: **Because by Your Holy Cross,**
           You have redeemed the world.

What a burden is laid on the shoulders of a man as he is
ordained — the weight of our sanctification, the obligation to
pray and suffer and sacrifice for our good — to do his part to
help fill up what is lacking in the sufferings of Christ for the
sake of His Church.[1]

Leader: Lord Jesus Crucified,
All: **Have mercy on all priests**.

THIRD STATION — Jesus Falls the First Time

Leader: We adore You, O Christ, and we praise You;

All: **Because by Your Holy Cross,
You have redeemed the world.**

What is it that caused Jesus to fall the first time? What causes a priest to fall? Could it be that there are so many demands on his time that he begins, little by little, to be torn away from his prayer life, his time with Jesus Who is the source of his strength? Prayer is his oxygen, the very life-breath of his priesthood.

Leader: Lord Jesus Crucified,
All: **Have mercy on all priests.**

**FOURTH STATION — Jesus Meets His Mother
on the Road to Calvary**

Leader: We adore You, O Christ, and we praise You;

All: **Because by Your Holy Cross,
You have redeemed the world.**

The sight of Mary consoled Jesus and yet increased His suffering because He knew how painful it was for Her to see Him this way.

How necessary it is that every priest look to Mary —
if only to turn his gaze upon Her from time to time each day
— and let Her motherly smile console and encourage him.

Leader: Lord Jesus Crucified,
All: **Have mercy on all priests..**

FIFTH STATION — Simon of Cyrene is Compelled to Help Jesus Carry His Cross

Leader: We adore You, O Christ, and we praise You;

All: **Because by Your Holy Cross,**
You have redeemed the world.

The word here is "compelled." St. Luke says Simon was "seized" and the Cross was "laid on him." [2]

The priest, one with Jesus, has come to the priesthood willing to embrace the Cross. How often, we, like Simon, have to be "compelled" to carry the Cross with Jesus, even "seized," and then we do so grudgingly.

Leader: Lord Jesus Crucified,
All: **Have mercy on all priests.**

2 *Luke 23:26 (RSV)*

THE LORD JESUS WIPES HIS FACE ON THE CLOAK OF VERONICA
VI

SIXTH STATION — Veronica Wipes the Face of Jesus

Leader: We adore You, O Christ, and we praise You;

All: **Because by Your Holy Cross,**
You have redeemed the world.

Veronica's name literally means "true icon" or "true image."

Every ordained priest, no matter who he is, where he is called to serve, or how he responds to that call, bears the true image of Christ — in his face, on his hands, on his very soul.

What can I do to imitate Veronica's kindness to the suffering Christ? What can I offer a suffering *alter Christus*?

Surely I can offer my prayers, perhaps a fast, perhaps an encouraging word or some other small kindness or sacrifice.

Leader: Lord Jesus Crucified,
All: **Have mercy on all priests.**

SEVENTH STATION — Jesus Falls a Second Time

Leader: We adore You, O Christ, and we praise You;

All: **Because by Your Holy Cross, You have redeemed the world.**

A second time, Jesus falls under the weight of the Cross.
He is exhausted and in unfathomable pain.

The priest who has been on his priestly journey for some time
must be constantly aware of the snares in his path lest he fall into
them. Of all these many pitfalls, perhaps the worst is loneliness
— for this one can lead him into a host of other dangers.

How very important it is that we pray for priests, especially
those who are lonely, and how vital it is that every priest has
the company and support of his brother priests. Above all,
the priest must immerse himself in Jesus Who alone satisfies,
fills the void of loneliness, heals wounds, gives strength, and
fills him with love.

Leader: Lord Jesus Crucified,
All: **Have mercy on all priests.**

THE LORD JESUS TURNS TO THE WEEPING WOMEN

VIII

EIGHTH STATION — Jesus Meets the Women of Jerusalem

Leader: We adore You, O Christ, and we praise You;

All: **Because by Your Holy Cross,**
You have redeemed the world.

Jesus, in spite of His pain and fatigue, stops to console others along His path.

How often the priest, weary, overwhelmed with responsibilities, struggling perhaps with his own pain, must reach out to ease the pain of others, to console and encourage, to be the mercy and compassion of Jesus at a deathbed, to redirect the course of a repentant sinner. And he may, in the midst of all this, feel acutely his own inadequacy. The road to Calvary is long and uphill.

Leader: Lord Jesus Crucified,
All: **Have mercy on all priests.**

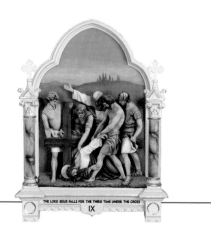

THE LORD JESUS FALLS FOR THE THIRD TIME UNDER THE CROSS

IX

NINTH STATION — Jesus Falls the Third Time

Leader: We adore You, O Christ, and we praise You;

All: **Because by Your Holy Cross,**
You have redeemed the world.

Jesus, near the end of His journey to Calvary, falls yet again. Surrounded by the brutality of the soldiers, He struggles to get up and keep going.

What caused Jesus to fall this third time? What might cause a priest to struggle and fall again and again? And how should we respond?

The priest is truly Jesus on the way to Calvary. When he falls under his burden, the gossip, unkindness and scorn he receives, in truth, fall on Jesus Who is suffering in His struggling brother priest.

Jesus could hear the mockery and scorn of those around Him and so can the priest. Will we love and pray a struggling priest back into service or let our words and actions keep him from getting up again?

Leader: Lord Jesus Crucified,
All: **Have mercy on all priests.**

THEY STRIP THE LORD JESUS AND GIVE HIM GALL TO DRINK

X

TENTH STATION — Jesus is Stripped of His Garments

Leader: We adore You, O Christ, and we praise You;

All: **Because by Your Holy Cross,**
You have redeemed the world.

Jesus' seamless tunic is stripped away from Him, causing His wounds to open and bleed. Naked and poor, His glory hidden, He stands before the crowd who does not recognize who He really is.

The priest, too, stands before the people — in sacred vestments, in black suit and collar, in places of honor. He is set apart from others. Still, when all this "covering" is taken away — when he is imprisoned by godless regimes and stripped of his freedom, when he has grown old and is stripped of his health and ability to serve, perhaps even when he has fallen into sin and is stripped of his own dignity — yet, he remains clothed in the sacred "garment" of the priesthood, and so shall he be for all eternity.

Leader: Lord Jesus Crucified,
All: **Have mercy on all priests.**

THEY NAIL THE LORD JESUS TO THE CROSS

XI

ELEVENTH STATION – Jesus is Nailed to the Cross

Leader: We adore You, O Christ, and we praise You;

All: **Because by Your Holy Cross,**
You have redeemed the world.

Jesus is nailed to the Cross. He hangs in agony, suspended between Heaven and Earth, suspended between two thieves — the one who reviles Him with disdain and the other who begs for mercy.

The priest, also nailed to the Cross by the very sacrificial nature of the priesthood, is suspended between Heaven, which he experiences in the Mass, and earth, which he experiences in the daily living out of his vocation. He, too, experiences those who revile and ridicule him and those who beg for mercy. United to Jesus, he must turn his gaze to the Father in Heaven.

Leader: Lord Jesus Crucified,
All: **Have mercy on all priests..**

THE LORD JESUS DIES ON THE CROSS
XII

TWELFTH STATION — Jesus Dies on the Cross

Leader: We adore You, O Christ, and we praise You;

All: **Because by Your Holy Cross,**
You have redeemed the world.

Jesus, having accomplished all that the Father sent Him to do,
says, "It is finished." [3]
"Father, into Your Hands I commend My Spirit." [4]

Every priest comes to his ordination day with a sense of
purpose and a desire to do the Will of the Father. And every
priest hopes to approach his death with a sense of having
accomplished all that he was given to do so that he may unite
himself with Jesus saying, "It is finished ... Father, into Your
Hands I commend my spirit."

Leader: Lord Jesus Crucified,
All: **Have mercy on all priests.**

3 John 19:30 (NAB)   4 Luke 23:46 (NAB)

THE BODY OF THE LORD JESUS IS TAKEN DOWN FROM THE CROSS

XIII

**THIRTEENTH STATION — The Body of Jesus is
Taken Down from the Cross
and Placed in the Arms
of His Mother**

Leader: We adore You, O Christ, and we praise You;

All: **Because by Your Holy Cross,
You have redeemed the world.**

Jesus' "hour" had finally come.[5] It will come for every priest,
too. And as Mary receives each priest as a special son on the
day of his ordination and remains at his side throughout his life
of ministry, so shall She receive into her arms every faithful son
at the hour of his death.

Leader: Lord Jesus Crucified,
All: **Have mercy on all priests.**

5 John 17:1 (NAB)

THE BODY OF THE LORD JESUS IS BROUGHT TO THE TOMB
XIV

FOURTEENTH STATION — Jesus is Laid in the Tomb

Leader: We adore You, O Christ, and we praise You;

All: **Because by Your Holy Cross,**
You have redeemed the world.

Jesus has completed His ministry on earth. By His Cross and Resurrection, He has set us free. He is the Savior of the World.

The priest, like Jesus, will go to the tomb someday.
Through the power of the Cross and Resurrection of Jesus,
he, too, through his ministry, has been able to set people
free — free from their sins, free to recognize Jesus as Savior,
free to enter into the Kingdom of God.

Leader: Lord Jesus Crucified,
All: **Have mercy on all priests.**

PRAYERS FOR THE HOLY FATHER

All: Our Father,
        Hail Mary,
        Glory Be

CONCLUDING PRAYER

All: Almighty and Eternal Father, we, Your children, lift up to You our prayers for our priests. We beg You to bless them and fill them with strength and perseverance as they take up their cross each day. Grant them to be faithful disciples of Christ the High Priest. Lead them as they lead us that we may all attain to eternal salvation. Grant this through Christ our Lord.

Amen.

THE RESURRECTION

APPENDIX A

Scripture Passages Grouped by Liturgical Season
All Scripture passages are quoted from the New American Bible

ADVENT SEASON — Option 1

A Reading from the Book of the Prophet Isaiah
(Isaiah 25:6-9)

On this mountain the LORD of hosts will provide for all peoples a feast of rich food and choice wines, juicy, rich food and pure, choice wines. On this mountain he will destroy the veil that veils all peoples, the web that is woven over all nations; he will destroy death forever. The Lord GOD will wipe away the tears from all faces; the reproach of his people he will remove from the whole earth; for the LORD has spoken.

On that day it will be said: "Behold our God, to whom we looked to save us! This is the LORD for whom we looked; let us rejoice and be glad that He has saved us!"

Leader: The Word of the Lord
All: **Thanks be to God.**

ADVENT SEASON – Option 2

A Reading from the Letter of St. Paul to the Romans
(Romans 1:1-7)

Paul, a slave of Christ Jesus, called to be an apostle and set apart for the gospel of God, which he promised previously through his prophets in the holy scriptures, the gospel about his Son, descended from David according to the flesh, but established as Son of God in power according to the spirit of holiness through resurrection from the dead, Jesus Christ our Lord.

Through him we have received the grace of apostleship, to bring about the obedience of faith, for the sake of his name, among all the Gentiles, among whom are you also, who are called to belong to Jesus Christ; to all the beloved of God in Rome, called to be holy. Grace to you and peace from God our Father and the Lord Jesus Christ.

Leader: The Word of the Lord
All: **Thanks be to God.**

CHRISTMAS SEASON – Option 1

A Reading from the Letter of St. Paul to the Colossians
(Colossians 1:15-29)

He is the image of the invisible God, the firstborn of all creation. For in him were created all things in heaven and on earth, the visible and the invisible, whether thrones or dominions or principalities or powers; all things were created through him and for him. He is before all things, and in him all things hold together. He is the head of the body, the church. He is the beginning, the firstborn from the dead, that in all things he himself might be preeminent. For in him all the fullness was pleased to dwell, and through him to reconcile all things for him, making peace by the blood of his cross [through him], whether those on earth or those in heaven.

And you who once were alienated and hostile in mind because of evil deeds he has now reconciled in his fleshly body through his death, to present you holy, without blemish, and irreproachable before him, provided that you persevere in the faith, firmly grounded, stable, and not shifting from the hope of the gospel that you heard, which has been preached to every creature under heaven, of which I, Paul, am a minister.

Now I rejoice in my sufferings for your sake, and in my flesh I am filling up what is lacking in the afflictions of Christ on behalf of his body, which is the Church, of which I am a minister in accordance with God's stewardship given to me to bring to completion for you the word of God, the mystery hidden from ages and from generations past. But now it has been manifested to his holy ones, to whom God chose to make known the riches of the glory of this mystery among the Gentiles; it is Christ in you, the hope for glory. It is he whom we proclaim, admonishing everyone and teaching everyone with all wisdom, that we may present everyone perfect in Christ. For this I labor and struggle, in accord with the exercise of his power working within me.

Leader: The Word of the Lord
All: **Thanks be to God.**

CHRISTMAS SEASON — Option 2

A Reading from the Book of the Prophet Isaiah
(Isaiah 62:6-12)

Upon your walls, O Jerusalem, I have stationed watchmen;
Never, by day or by night, shall they be silent. O you who are to
remind the Lord, take no rest and give no rest to him, until he
re-establishes Jerusalem and makes of it the pride of the earth.
The LORD has sworn by his right hand and by his mighty arm:
No more will I give your grain as food to your enemies; Nor
shall foreigners drink your wine, for which you toiled.
But you who harvest the grain shall eat it, and you shall praise
the LORD; you who gather the grapes shall drink the wine in
the courts of my sanctuary.

Pass through, pass through the gates, prepare the way for the
people; Build up, build up the highway, clear it of stones, raise
up a standard over the nations. See, the LORD proclaims to
the ends of the earth: Say to daughter Zion, your savior comes!
Here is his reward with him, his recompense before him. They
shall be called the holy people, the redeemed of the Lord, And
you shall be called "Frequented," a city that is not forsaken.

Leader: The Word of the Lord
All: **Thanks be to God.**

LENTEN SEASON – Option 1

A Reading from the Second Letter of St. Paul to the Corinthians
(2 Corinthians 5:17-6:10)

So whoever is in Christ is a new creation: the old things have passed away; behold, new things have come. And all this is from God, who has reconciled us to himself through Christ and given us the ministry of reconciliation, namely, God was reconciling the world to himself in Christ, not counting their trespasses against them and entrusting to us the message of reconciliation. So we are ambassadors for Christ, as if God were appealing through us. We implore you on behalf of Christ, be reconciled to God. For our sake he made him to be sin who did not know sin, so that we might become the righteousness of God in him.

Working together, then, we appeal to you not to receive the grace of God in vain. For he says:

"In an acceptable time I heard you, and on the day of salvation I helped you."

Behold, now is a very acceptable time; behold, now is the day of salvation. We cause no one to stumble in anything, in order that no fault may be found with our ministry; on the contrary, in everything we commend ourselves as ministers of God, through much endurance, in afflictions, hardships, constraints, beatings, imprisonments, riots, labors, vigils, fasts; by purity, knowledge, patience, kindness, in a holy spirit, in unfeigned love, in truthful

speech, in the power of God; with weapons of righteousness
at the right and at the left; through glory and dishonor, insult
and praise. We are treated as deceivers and yet are truthful;
as unrecognized and yet acknowledged; as dying and behold we
live; as chastised and yet not put to death; as sorrowful yet
always rejoicing; as poor yet enriching many; as having
nothing and yet possessing all things.

Leader: The Word of the Lord

All: **Thanks be to God.**

LENTEN SEASON — Option 2

A Reading from the Holy Gospel according to St. Luke
(Luke 22:14-20)

When the hour came, he took his place at table with the apostles.
He said to them, "I have eagerly desired to eat this Passover with
you before I suffer, for, I tell you, I shall not eat it [again] until there
is fulfillment in the kingdom of God." Then he took a cup, gave
thanks, and said, "Take this and share it among yourselves; for I tell
you [that] from this time on I shall not drink of the fruit of the vine
until the kingdom of God comes." Then he took the bread, said
the blessing, broke it, and gave it to them, saying, "This is my body,
which will be given for you; do this in memory of me." And likewise
the cup after they had eaten, saying, "This cup is the new covenant
in my blood, which will be shed for you."

Priest: The Gospel of the Lord

All: **Praise to you, Lord Jesus Christ**

EASTER SEASON — Option 1

A Reading from the Holy Gospel according to St. Luke
(Luke 24:13-35)

Now that very day two of them were going to a village seven miles from Jerusalem called Emmaus, and they were conversing about all the things that had occurred. And it happened that while they were conversing and debating, Jesus himself drew near and walked with them, but their eyes were prevented from recognizing him. He asked them, "What are you discussing as you walk along?" They stopped, looking downcast. One of them, named Cleopas, said to him in reply, "Are you the only visitor to Jerusalem who does not know of the things that have taken place there in these days?" And he replied to them, "What sort of things?" They said to him, "The things that happened to Jesus the Nazarene, who was a prophet mighty in deed and word before God and all the people, how our chief priests and rulers both handed him over to a sentence of death and crucified him. But we were hoping that he would be the one to redeem Israel; and besides all this, it is now the third day since this took place. Some women from our group, however, have astounded us: they were at the tomb early in the morning and did not find his body; they came back and reported that they had indeed seen a vision of angels who announced that he was alive. Then some of those with us went to the tomb and found things just as the women had described, but him they did not see." And he said to them, "Oh, how foolish you are! How slow of heart to believe all that the prophets spoke! Was it not necessary that the Messiah should suffer these things and enter into his glory?" Then beginning with Moses and all the prophets, he interpreted to them what referred to him in all the scriptures.

As they approached the village to which they were going, he gave the impression that he was going on farther. But they urged him, "Stay with us, for it is nearly evening and the day is almost over." So he went in to stay with them. And it happened that, while he was with them at table, he took bread, said the blessing, broke it, and gave it to them. With that their eyes were opened and they recognized him, but he vanished from their sight. Then they said to each other, "Were not our hearts burning [within us] while he spoke to us on the way and opened the scriptures to us?" So they set out at once and returned to Jerusalem where they found gathered together the eleven and those with them who were saying, "The Lord has truly been raised and has appeared to Simon!" Then the two recounted what had taken place on the way and how he was made known to them in the breaking of the bread.

Priest: The Gospel of the Lord
All: **Praise to you, Lord Jesus Christ**

EASTER SEASON – Option 2

A Reading from the Holy Gospel according to St. John
(John 20:19-23)

On the evening of that first day of the week, when the doors were locked, where the disciples were, for fear of the Jews, Jesus came and stood in their midst and said to them, "Peace be with you." When he had said this, he showed them his hands and his side. The disciples rejoiced when they saw the Lord.
[Jesus] said to them again, "Peace be with you. As the Father has sent me, so I send you." And when he had said this, he breathed on them and said to them, "Receive the holy Spirit. Whose sins you forgive are forgiven them, and whose sins you retain are retained."

Priest: The Gospel of the Lord

All: **Praise to you, Lord Jesus Christ**

EASTER SEASON – Option 3

A Reading from the Holy Gospel according to St. John
(John 21:15-19)

When they had finished breakfast, Jesus said to Simon Peter, "Simon, son of John, do you love me more than these?" He said to him, "Yes, Lord, you know that I love you." He said to him, "Feed My lambs." He then said to him a second time, "Simon, son of John, do you love me?" He said to him, "Yes, Lord, you know that I love you." He said to him, "Tend my sheep." He said to him the third time, "Simon, son of John, do you love me?" Peter was distressed that he had said to him a third time, "Do you love me?" and he said to him, "Lord, you know everything; you know that I love you." [Jesus] said to him, "Feed my sheep. Amen, amen, I say to you, when you were younger, you used to dress yourself and go where you wanted; but when you grow old, you will stretch out your hands, and someone else will dress you and lead you where you do not want to go." He said this signifying by what kind of death he would glorify God. And when he had said this, he said to him, "Follow me."

Priest: The Gospel of the Lord

All: **Praise to you, Lord Jesus Christ**

ORDINARY TIME – Option 1

A Reading from the Book of Genesis
(Genesis 14:18-20)

Melchizedek, king of Salem, brought out bread and wine, and being a priest of God Most High, he blessed Abram with these words: "Blessed be Abram by God Most High, the creator of heaven and earth; And blessed be God Most High, who delivered your foes into your hand." Then Abram gave him a tenth of everything.

Leader: The Word of the Lord
All: **Thanks be to God.**

ORDINARY TIME – Option 2

A Reading from the Letter to the Hebrews
(Hebrews 4:14-5:10)

Therefore, since we have a great high priest who has passed through the heavens, Jesus, the Son of God, let us hold fast to our confession. For we do not have a high priest who is unable to sympathize with our weaknesses, but one who has similarly been tested in every way, yet without sin. So let us confidently approach the throne of grace to receive mercy and to find grace for timely help.

Every high priest is taken from among men and made their representative before God, to offer gifts and sacrifices for sins. He is able to deal patiently with the ignorant and erring, for he himself is beset by weakness and so, for this reason, must make sin offerings for himself as well as for the people. No one takes this honor upon himself but only when called by God, just as Aaron was.

In the same way, it was not Christ who glorified himself in becoming high priest, but rather the one who said to him:

"You are my son; this day I have begotten you";
just as he says in another place:

"You are a priest forever according to the order of Melchizedek."

In the days when he was in the flesh, he offered prayers and supplications with loud cries and tears to the one who was able to save him from death, and he was heard because of his reverence. Son though he was, he learned obedience from what he suffered; and when he was made perfect, he became the source of eternal salvation for all who obey him, declared by God high priest according to the order of Melchizedek.

Leader: The Word of the Lord
All: **Thanks be to God.**

ORDINARY TIME — Option 3

A Reading from the Holy Gospel according to St. Mark
(Mark 10:42-45)

Jesus summoned them and said to them, "You know that those who are recognized as rulers over the Gentiles lord it over them, and their great ones make their authority over them felt. But it shall not be so among you. Rather, whoever wishes to be great among you will be your servant; whoever wishes to be first among you will be the slave of all. For the Son of Man did not come to be served but to serve and to give his life as a ransom for many."

Priest: The Gospel of the Lord

All: **Praise to you, Lord Jesus Christ**

ORDINARY TIME — Option 4

A Reading from the First Letter of St. Paul to Timothy
(1 Timothy 6:6-16)

Indeed, religion with contentment is a great gain. For we brought nothing into the world, just as we shall not be able to take anything out of it. If we have food and clothing, we shall be content with that. Those who want to be rich are falling into temptation and into a trap and into many foolish and harmful desires, which plunge them into ruin and destruction. For the love of money is the root of all evils, and some people in their desire for it have strayed from the faith and have pierced themselves with many pains.

But you, man of God, avoid all this. Instead, pursue righteousness, devotion, faith, love, patience, and gentleness. Compete well for the faith. Lay hold of eternal life, to which you were called when you made the noble confession in the presence of many witnesses.

I charge [you] before God, who gives life to all things, and before Christ Jesus, who gave testimony under Pontius Pilate for the noble confession, to keep the commandment without stain or reproach until the appearance of our Lord Jesus Christ that the blessed and only ruler will make manifest at the proper time, the King of kings and Lord of lords, who alone has immortality, who dwells in unapproachable light, and whom no human being has seen or can see. To him be honor and eternal power. Amen.

Leader: The Word of the Lord
All: **Thanks be to God.**

ORDINARY TIME – Option 5

A Reading from the Second Letter of St. Paul to Timothy
(2 Timothy 4:1-8)

I charge you in the presence of God and of Christ Jesus, who will judge the living and the dead, and by his appearing and his kingly power: proclaim the word; be persistent whether it is convenient or inconvenient; convince, reprimand, encourage through all patience and teaching. For the time will come when people will not tolerate sound doctrine but, following their own desires and insatiable curiosity, will accumulate teachers and will stop listening to the truth and will be diverted to myths. But you, be self-possessed in all circumstances; put up with hardship; perform the work of an evangelist; fulfill your ministry.

For I am already being poured out like a libation, and the time of my departure is at hand. I have competed well; I have finished the race; I have kept the faith. From now on the crown of righteousness awaits me, which the Lord, the just judge, will award to me on that day, and not only to me, but to all who have longed for his appearance.

Leader: The Word of the Lord
All: **Thanks be to God.**

ORDINARY TIME — Option 6

A Reading from the First Letter of St. Peter
(1 Peter 5:1-4, 8-11)

So I exhort the presbyters among you, as a fellow presbyter and witness to the sufferings of Christ and one who has a share in the glory to be revealed. Tend the flock of God in your midst, [overseeing] not by constraint but willingly, as God would have it, not for shameful profit but eagerly. Do not lord it over those assigned to you, but be examples to the flock. And when the chief Shepherd is revealed, you will receive the unfading crown of glory.

Be sober and vigilant. Your opponent the devil is prowling around like a roaring lion looking for [someone] to devour. Resist him, steadfast in faith, knowing that your fellow believers throughout the world undergo the same sufferings. The God of all grace who called you to his eternal glory through Christ [Jesus] will himself restore, confirm, strengthen, and establish you after you have suffered a little. To him be dominion forever.

Amen.

Leader: The Word of the Lord
All: **Thanks be to God.**

WORKS CITED

Catholic Church, Directory on the Life and Ministry of Priests.
Vatican City: *Libreria Editrice Vaticana*, 1994.

Catholic Church, *Rosarium Virginis Mariae*.
Vatican City: *Libreria Editrice Vaticana*, 2002.

Diary of St. Maria Faustina Kowalska:
Divine Mercy in My Soul © 1987 Congregation of Marians
of the Immaculate Conception, Stockbridge, MA 01263.
Used with permission.

New American Bible, St. Joseph's Edition. New York, NY:
Catholic Book Publishing, 1992.

Ignatius Bible, Revised Standard Version. San Francisco, CA:
Ignatius Press, Catholic Edition of the New Testament,
Copyright 1965; Catholic Edition of the Old Testament,
incorporating the Apocrypha, 1966.

Serra Prayer for Vocations. USA Council of Serra International.
Used with permission.

REFERENCES

Parts I and II

1 Hebrews 7:17 (NAB*)

2 Luke 2:25 (NAB)

3 Luke 2:34 (NAB)

4 Luke 2:52 (NAB)

5 *Rosarium Virginis Mariae*, 21

6 John 1:29 (NAB)

7 John 2:3 (NAB)

8 John 2:5 (NAB)

9 Mark 1:15 (NAB)

10 Luke 22:42 (RSV†)

11 Isaiah 53:3,7 (RSV)

12 Matthew 28:19 (NAB)

13 Directory on the Ministry and Life of Priests, 9

14 John 19:26 (NAB)

15 Divine Mercy in My Soul, (Diary, #1052)
Diary of St. Maria Faustina Kowalska:
Divine Mercy in My Soul © 1987 Congregation of Marians
of the Immaculate Conception, Stockbridge, MA 01263.
Used with permission.

Stations of the Cross

1 Colossians 1:24 (NAB)

2 Luke 23:26 (RSV)

3 John 19:30 (NAB)

4 Luke 23:46 (NAB)

5 John 17:1 (NAB)

ORDERING INFORMATION

Please order copies of this book
for yourself, your parish, prayer group,
or any other organization that wishes
to pray for our priests.

Simply visit our Web site at:

www.prayingforourpriests.org

GOD BLESS YOU!